Great Country Store Antiques

Rich Bertoia

Schiffer Publishing Ltd

4880 Lower Valley Road, Atglen, PA 19310 USA

Copyright © 2001 by Rich Bertoia
Library of Congress Card Number: 00-107440

Designed by Bonnie M. Hensley
Cover Design by Bruce M. Waters
Type set in Bernard BdCn BT/Korinna BT

ISBN: 0-7643-1236-7
Printed in China
1 2 3 4

Published by Schiffer Publishing Ltd.
4880 Lower Valley Road
Atglen, PA 19310
Phone: (610) 593-1777; Fax: (610) 593-2002
E-mail: Schifferbk@aol.com
Please visit our web site catalog at **www.schifferbooks.com**

In Europe, Schiffer books are distributed by Bushwood Books
6 Marksbury Avenue Kew Gardens
Surrey TW9 4JF England
Phone: 44 (0) 20-8392-8585; Fax: 44 (0) 20-8392-9876
E-mail: Bushwd@aol.com
Free postage in the UK. Europe: air mail at cost.

This book may be purchased from the publisher.
Include $3.95 for shipping. Please try your bookstore first.
We are always looking for people to write books on new and related subjects.
If you have an idea for a book please contact us at the above address.
You may write for a free catalog.

Contents

Acknowledgments

Bob Lyons may have just set out to collect what he liked, but along the way, he single handedly helped preserve a small piece of the real American story. Anyone who tours through this book, or the others that will follow, will come to appreciate the discriminating eye of one of the great collectors of our time. I certainly can't thank Bob enough for his years of gathering such a masterpiece of Americana under one roof, and for allowing me to do this book. In a way that only Bob can, he has shown me true friendship and constant enthusiasm.

My thanks to my brother Bill Bertoia, for introducing me to Bob, and for suggesting the idea of further preserving the country store images in a book, or two, or three.

A big share of gratitude and applause goes to master motivator, and unselfish publisher, Mr. Peter Schiffer. His enthusiasm was also overwhelming, and always welcomed. Peter's team also receives high honors for their tremendous photo portrayals of the collection. It was a huge undertaking, and their professionalism is evident on every page. Organized by Doug Congdon-Martin, photographers Bruce Waters and Blair Loughrey, together with recorders Jennifer Lindbeck and Donna Baker, have helped put this book in motion. This is team work at its best, and they deserve a loud "job well done."

I must, of course, thank my daughters, Nina, Lani, and Monica, for giving up their valuable computer time, and letting dad pretend to act computer literate for a while, and my wife Trina for her constant supply of coffee on many late nights. Honorable mention goes to "Cyber Bob" Carr, of Bertoia Auctions, for mentoring my computing skills, and to the entire staff at Bertoia's for unending support. Lastly, my father, Hector Bertoia, for his encouraging and effective intermittent remark throughout this project, "Start writing – I can't wait to read it."

Preface

The Bob Lyons Country Store

Some people dream of gathering a sizeable collection of country store items, but rarely does one imagine owning his own authentic country store. However, in a true labor of love, Bob Lyons of Ypsilanti, Michigan, turned his dream into reality and assembled a genuine country store, which is proudly displayed in the pages of this book. It's a major achievement in the annals of collecting. The quality and originality of Bob's country store can be equaled only if one were to go back, say, ninety years ago or so, and walk through a small town in rural America. In fact, when visiting Bob's store today, you get a feeling that time has allowed you to cheat it for a moment and glimpse into its past. It becomes a refreshingly simple look at how and where common folk shopped before the days of the super malls and discount stores.

Bob has assembled a complete country store that can be appreciated by all of us for its historical value and for its preservation of a slice of early American life. The importance of the store is brought together by the quantity and quality of items displayed within, creating a time capsule in Americana. Amassing such a collection to outfit the store would be an almost impossible task today, but Bob's advantage was perfect timing, having started well over twenty-five years ago, which partnered his very discriminating eye for great collectibles. He traveled extensively in the pursuit of rare items to complement his inventory, and the variety and completeness of the sort makes it one of the finest privately owned displays ever put together.

Bob has cordially led many people through his country store over the years, and he has never tired of the surprised reactions it receives. The country store has provided Bob with a true haven of relaxation, as it is located only steps away from his business office, and Bob's humble reward has been years of enjoyment in sharing his hobby with appreciative antique buffs.

This book attempts to individualize portions of the store to better capture a complete pictorial view of the collection. The enormous task of recording this store on film will be appreciated by viewers who wish, as I did, to study what can almost be referred to as a true American archeological find.

I am both pleased and proud to have been part of this huge project, and all the photographs involved will forever share in the book's glory and importance.

Mr. Lyons has in essence become and architect of the finest collection known, and I hope you enjoy this lasting version of his blueprints in photos.

Introduction

More than Just a Place to Shop

The country store was more then just a place to shop; it was a place to exchange local gossip, catch first hand news on community politics, and, oh yes, shop for the latest in food items, kitchen gadgetry, and fashion apparel. The country store was the meeting place of the town's elite and of the average working family. One can only sense the excitement of the country store's newly advertised products. At a time of such industrial growth, keeping up with the Joneses must have been very difficult indeed.

The country store contained many of those new and improved products that were to revolutionize the way people ate, dressed, and managed a daily existence. But in order to attract customers to the ever-changing way of life, the storeowner had to wear many hats in his operation. His job not only entailed keeping up with the latest in merchandise, but, more importantly, keeping an alluring presentation of his goods to the town's captive audience. Showcases had to be placed in a user-friendly layout without any wasted space for stale goods.

Counter displays had to magnetize the attention of the impulse buyer, canned goods had to be arranged in an eye pleasing grouping, just asking to be plucked away and taken home, and the new fashions had to be paraded in full sight of those seeking to dress for success. The storekeeper became the answer man, part time psychologist, interior decorator, fashion consultant, and generally the big brother for the entire community. He, or she, as the case may have been, was at times, the only link between a city slicker salesman and the American mainstream. People entrusted the storekeeper to sell them the latest of styles and house wares, and children usually found his store a favorite stop over for the best in sweets.

The country store reflects a time in America when life was simple, and people liked it that way. A simple checkers table was the most important item in the store because controlling a space at the table meant you could see who was shopping for what, and never miss a juicy bit of town news. Its charm still beguiles us today.

Chapter One

Showcasing the Country Store

While impulsive buying may have been rooted in the glittering lit streets and shops of the big cities, the country store was, for many people, the only place to spend quality shopping time, a little bit of hard earned money, and buy all the necessities of every day life, including whatever caught the eye. Shopkeepers knowing this, created their own methods of luring indecisive buyers to buy the needed and the unneeded items of the day. With the contribution of showcase manufacturers adding the finishing touches to help present goods at their best, the country store was made to feel as inviting and exciting as a stroll to Saks Fifth Avenue must have felt for a wealthy New York shopper.

Showcases, which generally lined the walls and covered most of area of the store, were normally made of rich oak with large panels of glass for easy viewing and easy maintenance, ensuring a gleaming attractiveness to the displayed goods. Many of the early cases had large brass company plates placed on corners or centered in plain sight, further adding to the elegance of the cabinet and importance of the displayed items. With a high-polished look and fully stocked shelves, the country store attempted to imitate the big city store with the charm of casual and old-fashioned surroundings. People were not intimidated over entering and asking questions about new products never before introduced to the town; this surely made a trip to the store a very special part of ordinary life. The following chapters demonstrate the diversity of country store furnishings, and the captivating displays.

An inviting look at a well-stocked country store display case. The props and advertisements surrounding the display helped catch the eye and hold the attention of a curious customer. Montreal Show Case Co., Montreal, Que. Wood, glass, metal trim. 30" x 66" x 27". $1200-1500

An enormous display case, which could fill a sidewall nicely. The clothing could be easily inspected by customers, and it gave the storekeeper plenty of room to show off the latest city styles. Claes & Lehnbeuter, St. Louis, Mo. Oak with metal trim. 43" x 117" x 28". $2000-2500

Large multi-unit display case. Perfect for the country store walls, and built with true skill and craftsmanship. These solid oak units are very desirable, allowing room to walk around and view, with the added luxury of pull-out drawers for flat collectibles. 95" x 72" (each unit) x 24". $2000-2500. Additional matching side units make this even more valuable.

Note the added trim to this peaked case. The products must have certainly seemed high quality if housed in such a magnificent cabinet. Display case (tobacco). H. Kruse & Co., 86 & 88 Main Street, Cincinnati, Ohio. Oak, glass, metal trim. 41" x 27" x 24". $1500-2000.

A larger peaked cabinet with a prominent look and wide curved glass front for total visibility of goods. The mirrored backdrop, common in many early cabinets, gave the illusion of large depth and size to a sometimes small store. Nashville Showcase Co. Nashville, Tenn. Oak and glass, with mirrored inset. 66" x 59" x 28". $2500-3000

A storekeeper had a full time job keeping his display cabinets this well and neatly stocked. Display cabinet. Jos. Knittel Showcase Co., Quincy, Ill., Branch St. Louis. Oak and glass. 30" x 27.5" x 16".

Imagine the thrill of seeking the latest in fancy threads from this extraordinary cabinet. Thread cabinet, mirrored on sides. Oak. 48" x 35" x 17". $2500-3500

Bin type cabinets were very useful for food or spices. They remind us of today's bulk shops or the convenience "help yourself" store. Walnut and glass. 27" x 61" x 26". Depending on number of bins, $1500-2500

A full view of the country store supermarket. Grain counter, "The Sherer Counter." Sher Gillette Co., Chicago, Ill., Patented 1911, Serial # 40520. 33.5" x 144" x 28.5".

A shopper's view of the thread selection. Thread cabinet. "Corlielli Spool Silk & Twist." Oak. 53" x 49.5" x 18.5".

Easily tucked in a corner of the store, but very practical, some were built like today's lazy Susans in our kitchen cabinets. Octagonal hardware cabinet. Oak. 44" x 11" (each side). $2200-2700.

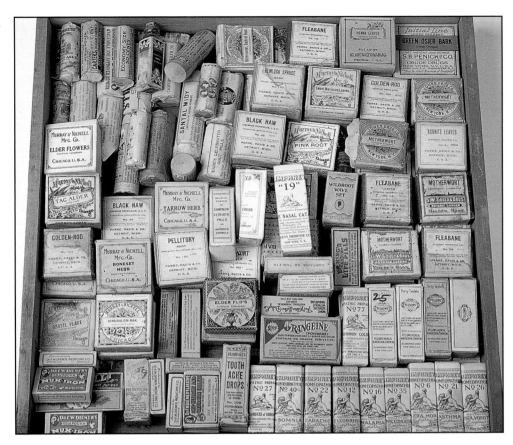

Storekeepers optimized space, as evidence by these two pull-out drawers from within the cabinets. Pictured contents include assorted pharmaceutical products, including herbal and homeopathic products, toothache drops, Carter's Little Nervine Pills, Dr. Hobson's Pink Pain pills, laxatives for adults and children, and corn removers.

Spice cabinet counter tops served a useful purpose for measuring reams of linen or displaying assorted trinkets such as toys.

The drugs were usually kept in display cabinets with marble tops. This allowed the storekeeper to appear more professional and gave him a hygienic area to dispense the latest remedies without the clutter of food, candy, or fertilizer. These cabinets normally came with fancy gold script and extra heavy wooden doors to keep out the stale air of the store. Wooden display cabinet with drawers, "Sterilizer." 25" x 36" x 9.5". $2200-2700

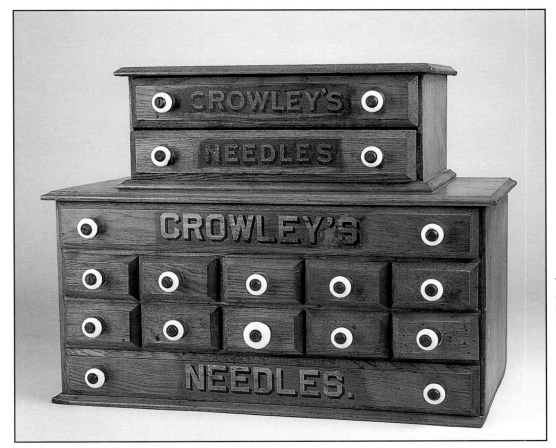

A store owner must have felt proud to show if this highly ornate drug case. The trappings displayed by Mr. Lyons are perfect compliments and depict an exacting picture of the early country store. Walnut and glass. 40" x 67" x 24". $4000+

Wooden needle chest with drawers, complete with attention grabbing porcelain knobs and large gold lettering. 15" x 18" x 9.75". $3000-3500

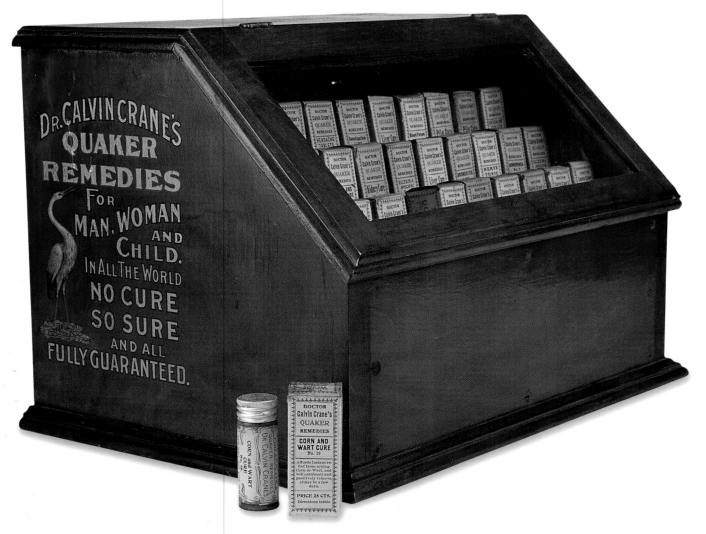

Easy to shop for medicines with this glass front cabinet. Counter display of various patented medicines. Side label "Guaranteed under the food and drug act, June 30th, 1906, Serial number 9903." $2000-2500

Impressive, yet fully functional, taking up little precious space in the store. Display rack for canes. The A. H. Revell Mfg. Co., 431-437 5th Ave., Chicago, Ill. Oak and glass. 48" x 24" x 14.5". $1750-2500

Another display rack for canes, this one ready for a new shipment. Alex H. Revell & Co., 431-437 5th Ave., Chicago, Ill. 48" x 24.5" x 26".

Behind this fabulous "Test Your Strength" machine, stands a great multi drawer cabinet used for countless objects. The machine is made of cast iron and wood. 59" high. Cabinet's value $2500-3000.

In addition to making the country store appear inviting and allowing goods to be displayed in plain sight, the larger glass front showcases also gave the storekeeper a great area to display the many fancy and colorful table top cabinets given out by salesmen for use with their product lines. The earlier versions were made mostly of wood and glass, but tin lithographed versions eventually flooded the market. The colorful graphics made a cheap and effective way to advertise a product, and having one in a high traffic area must have cost a favor or two from the keeper, but well worth the returns. The Bob Lyons store contains an excellent representation of wood and tin display cases, and the following examples form an integral part of the collection.

Multi-level display cabinet for Clark's "Anchor" Stranded Cotton for Embroidery. Oak and glass. 6.25" x 22" x 7.5". $300-400

Ornately fashioned thread display cabinet. Sure to draw as much attention as the interior products. Merrick's Spool Cotton. Patented July 20, 1897. Oak and glass with mirrored front panel. 23.5" x 25".

Note that the wording reads "loaned," Many of the cabinets were returned if found not to bring in good profits or if there were a trademark change. In any event, it seemed that the companies could use this ploy as leverage for retrieval if not displayed in a prominent location or used for other products by the store owner. Wooden display cabinet for Boye brand sewing needles. Marked on reverse: "This cabinet is loaned for display and sale of 'Boye' merchandise only. The Boye Needle Company, New York - Chicago - San Francisco. Cabinet Style 1 Pat. Appd. For." 11.5" x 12" x 7". $500-800

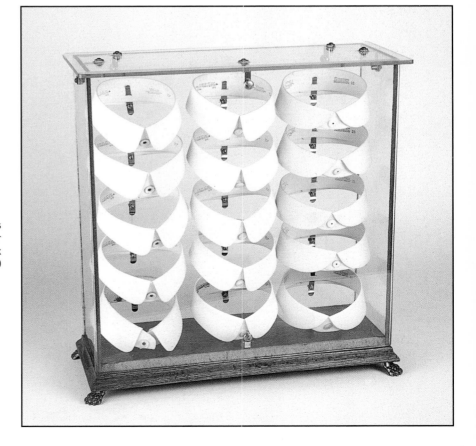

Display case for men's collars. Choosing from this cabinet must have made any gentleman feel rather important. Three row, glass with wood base. 20" x 19" x 6.5". $750-900

Display rack for Bissell carpet sweepers with detail photo of the elaborate sweepers themselves, "Cyco Bearing." 53" x 31.5". $600-750

Tiered display cabinet. This may have had multi display uses for jewelry or even delectable candies Wood and glass paneled. 31.5" x 13.75" x 13.75". $400-600

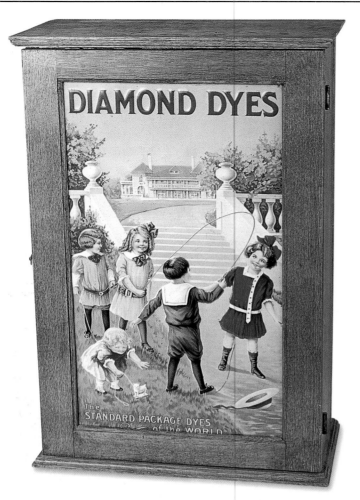

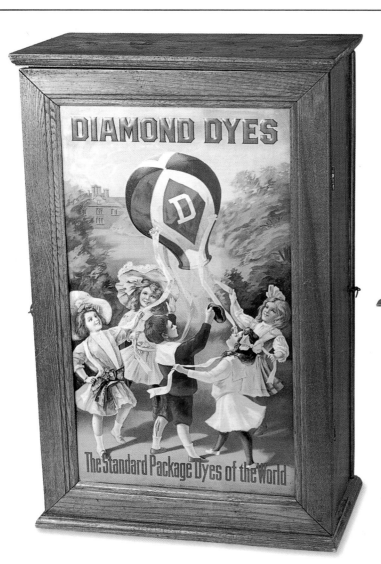

Dyes were part of life in the nineteenth century and the following photos depict a series of dye cabinets produced for Diamond Dyes Co. These are very popular with collectors and are becoming increasingly difficult to find. Diamond Package Dyes, made by Wells & Richardson Co., Burlington, Vermont and Montreal, Canada. Pine and Oak examples. 29.5" x 23" x 9". $1500+

Cabinet for Diamond Dyes, shown with interior slots for dye packages and instruction booklets inside. 24" x 15.25" x 7.5".

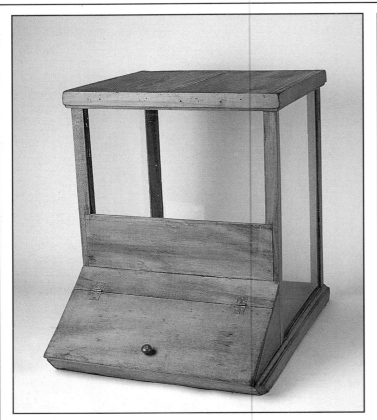 

These showcases were familiar sights to shoppers of earlier times. Each was fashioned for optimum display and space-saving symmetry. Goods contained within the shelves included baked items, teas, or candies. The tall case was built to highlight a large item or, with shelves installed, many of the day's goodies. Prices for these will vary according to amount of trim work, enhanced lettering, and, of course, size. Collectors prefer a trade name or article title on the cabinet, and this can affect the price by hundreds of dollars alone.

A great visual display piece with a real take-me-home look. Lithographed tin coffee display for Johnson's Log Cabin Coffee.25" x 24" x 13". $5000

After choosing from the display case, a handy bag holder was the needed rack . "Mack's Fancy Bag Rack." Wood with cast iron string holder on top. 20" x 11.5" x 13.5". $500

This was an imaginative advertising display unit which surely caught much attention. Ginger Ale display, Saegertown Old Style Ginger Ale. Bottled by The Saegertown Mineral Water Co., Saegertown, PA., copyright 1919". $400-600, with original bottles the price increases

Even shoe laces were given special graphic appeal as demonstrated by this popular lithographed tin Shoe Lace Service Station. Woodlawn Mills. Lithographed tin. 14" x 11.5" x 11". $1750-2000

The vegetables were fresh and, just like today's stores, always at hand for squeezing inspection. Vegetable bin. Painted wire and an example with added wood base. 36" x 35" x 15". Many examples are found with varying wire patterns. These are rather fancy and increase the value substantially. $750+

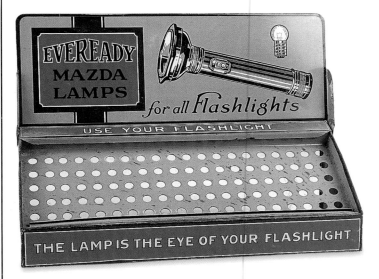

The following entries form part of the tin lithographed assortment of fanciful counter top displays. Literally thousands of these rich graphic examples exist The popularity is found in the unique products or in the design of the display itself. Pictured are displays for batteries, cigars, candy, sparkplugs, razor blades, and tobacco. A country store was probably rated by the quality of its tobacco products, and any quality store carried an ample supply for the men of the community. Similar displays have recently sold for $400-900.

More examples of the magic of tin lithography for various products. Multi level units made great space saving use while creating a dramatic display. The round Java tin is an early example that was a common sight at a fully stocked country store. The images are quite elaborate and give an air of quality to the product. Prices vary according to artwork and quality of stenciling. Patriotic themes command unusually high figures, and are extremely rare.

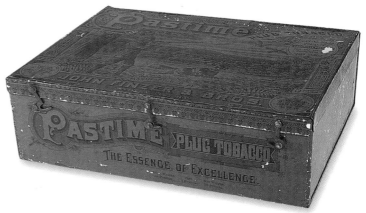

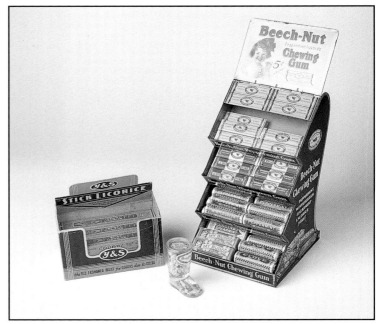

Display case for Lister's Imperial Silks. This case with bright gold lettering is one of the predecessors of the tin litho variety. Tin graphics made it much easier to call attention with multi-colored patterns. 16" x 12" x 12". $500-750

Another medium for the country store shelves. Milk glass display with packs of Wrigley's Spearmint and Juicy Fruit gum. Glass case marked "The Pflugradt Co., Milwaukee, Wis.," 15.5" x 9". $500-600

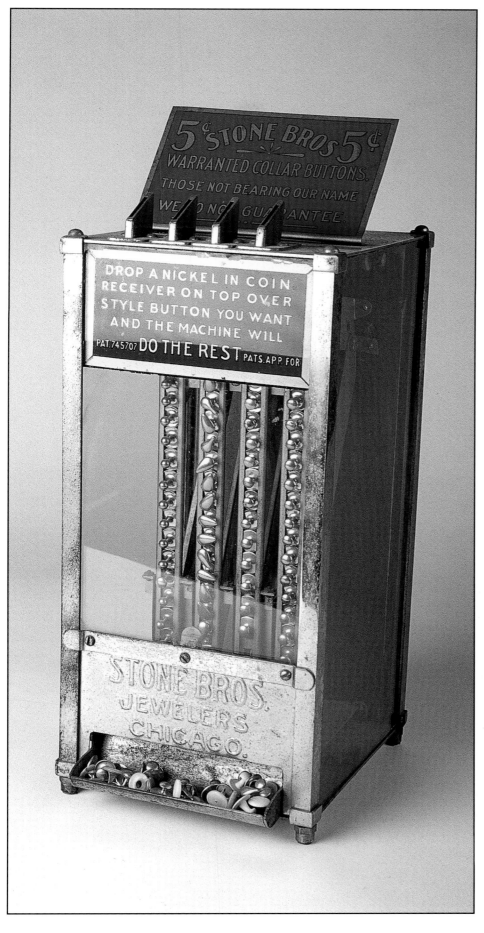

A different sort of coin-op dispenser. This one dispensed collar buttons, marked "Pat. 745707, Pat. App. For." Stone Bros. Jewelers, Chicago. 16.25" x 6.25" x 7". $600-800

While mom and the children were busy shopping, dad could entertain himself with these fabulous and amusing. coin-op trade stimulators. Above is a coin-op with a bicycle theme. Oak, glass, and metal. 13.5" x 19" x 5". The coin-op on the facing page is called "Fairest Wheel," Pat. May 7, 1895. Decatur Fairest Wheel Works, Decatur, Ill. Oak, glass, and metal. 21" x 15". At the right is "The Bicycle Wheel," advertising "The Best 5c Cigar in the House." Waddel W. W. Works, Greenfield, Ohio. Oak, glass, and metal. 20" x 15.5" x 3.5". $900+

What better way to view the grand store or maybe bargain with the owner to take one home. These early kerosene fueled hanging lamps must have cast a tremendous light. Tiered kerosene chandelier. Metal and glass. Approx. 30" to 45" diameter. Unique items like these in mint condition are difficult to price.

More merchandise that could be selected from the counter tops. From the common match to the latest in Ford Dash Lamps, the country store begins to reveal its total worth for a community located miles from city life. The unusual tobacco item was billed as the "The Prince of Vending Machines." Just like the big city stores and surely a popular counter item. Universal Vending Machine, Co., Battle Creek, Mich. Cast iron. 11" x 13" x 7".

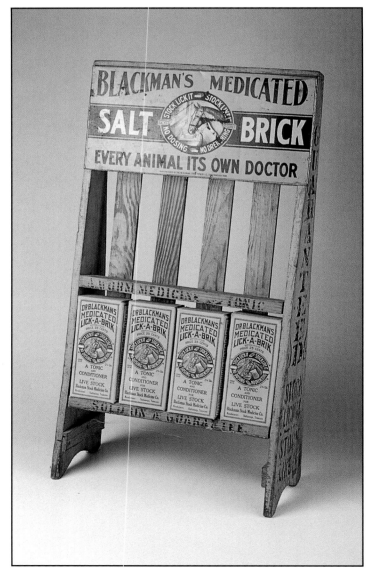

Chapter Two

Open for Business

A fully stocked country store carried everything from common necessities to the extravagant and latest in household inventions. The shelves poured over with canned goods needed for survival and gadgets useful in making daily chores a little less tiring for the keeper. Many of these implements proved unworthy for ease of use while others were simply modified over the years and are still a part of our daily lives today. The words "new and improved" appeared on countless items, demonstrating the fury of inventors to perfect ordinary goods, for the good of their pockets and, of course, the people that needed to use them.

The turn of the century was a time of inventive spirit comparable to the present computer tech race. Bob's country store features many of the unusual items that filled the fully stocked shelves of early marketplaces, and allows our curiosity to explore them first hand with fascinating close-up scrutiny. We begin the chapter by examining the tools of the store trade and a sample of a few of the goods used by pioneering Americans that formed our culture during the turn of the century. A storekeeper in Bob's country store would have been fully outfitted to serve his community and able to fill large or small orders with ease.

This handy bag rack, with top mounted string holder, was a space saver and must have seen plenty of action. 42" x 10" x 23.5". A unique item.

Setting up a proper shop meant having all the necessities of the store trade. In addition to sparkling cabinetry, the keeper was equipped with everything needed to ensure accurate measurements, weights, and final packaging. The most important tool of the trade was a magnificent cash register such as this one pictured. It was ornately and heavily cast to discourage someone from attempting to carry it away from the store. "The Seymour." Oak with nickel plate trim. 21.5" x 16.75" x 13.75". $1000-1500

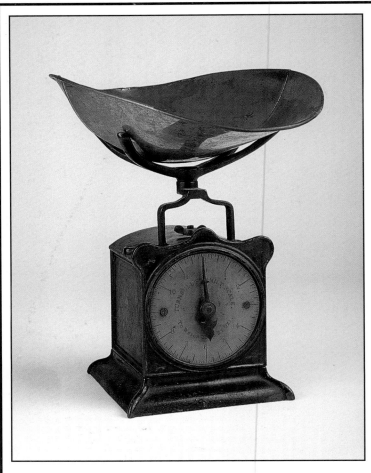

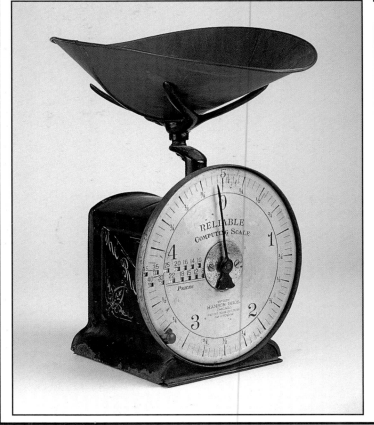

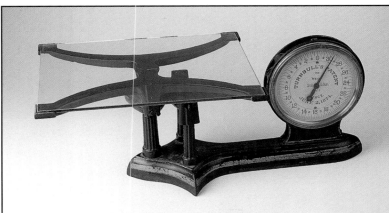

Scales for every job. These were used for candy, meats, flour, nails, and everything in between. The designs are endless and a scale made another fancy adornment to the countertop. Many of the smaller scales include company advertisements and are more desirable to collectors, making them easier to display. Prices vary widely, but they are generally found in the $100-500 range.

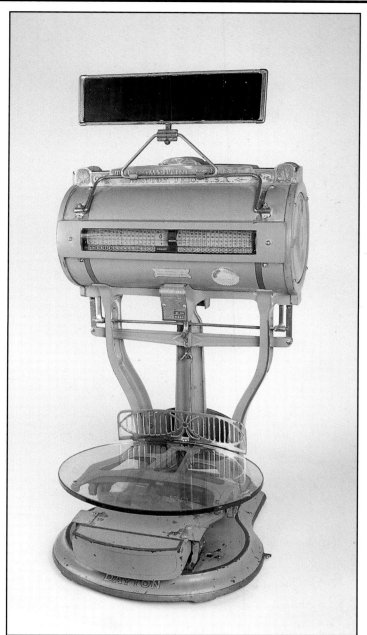

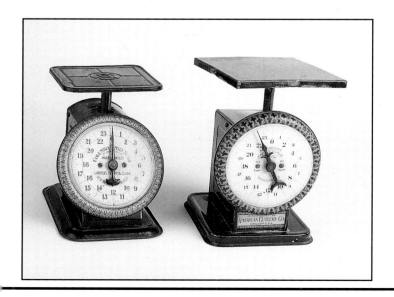

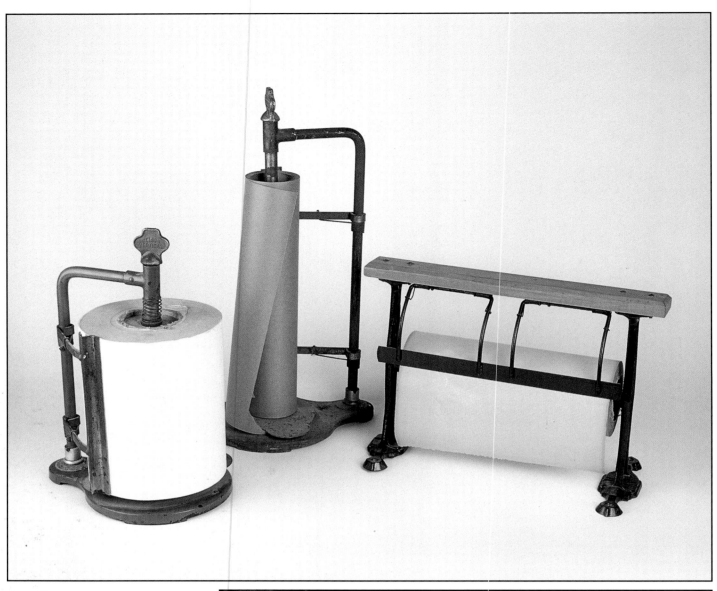

Three paper dispensers, assorted shapes. Wood and metal. $200-300

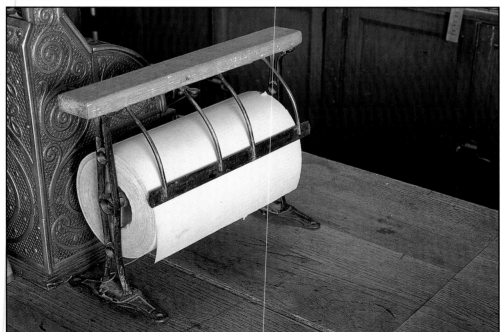

Conveniently placed next to cash register. Paper roll dispenser. Cast iron and wood. 12" x 16.5" x 7". $200

Another ornate paper dispenser, "Arrow." Cast iron and wood. 12.5" x 11". Collectors desire the unusual, and this cast iron model qualifies as unique. $300-400

Coffee grinder with roaster, "Royal." A. J. Deer Co., Inc. 51" x 36". NRS

Ornate cast iron coffee grinder. Usually found painted in red for counter visibility. The Swift Mill Lane Brothers, Poughkeepsie, New York. 35" x 16" x 22.5". $1500-2500

Coffee grinder with fine details and nickeled top. Star Mill, Philadelphia. Cast iron. 34. 5" high. $1500-1500

The storekeeper could easily sell a dozen eggs at a time from this handy egg crate. Owosso Mfg. Co. 13.5" x 12.5" x 12.5". $100-150

Spices were weighed and sold straight from the racks, just like bulk items are today. These are fancy store counter spice canisters, Allspice, Ginger, Pepper, Mustard, and Cream of Tartar. Lithographed tin. 11" x 8" x 7" each. $200-300

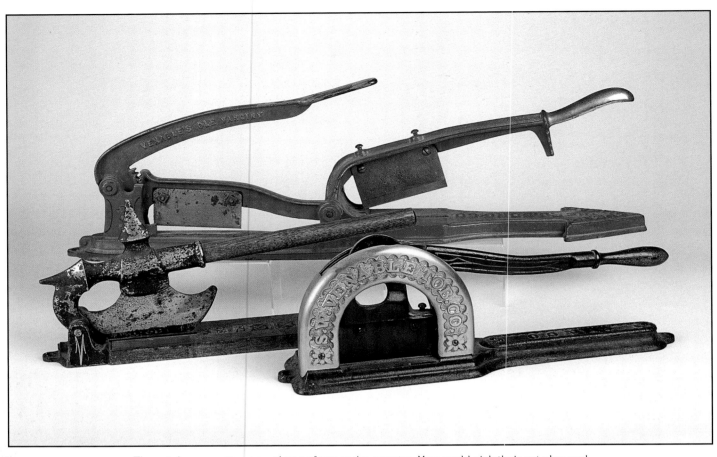

These tobacco cutters saw plenty of use at the counter. Men could pick their cut plug and have the keeper cut it into perfect size. Prices range from $75 to $300

A three foot wooden wheelbarrow was perfect for the store helper to carry feed bags to a customer's waiting wagon. $200-250

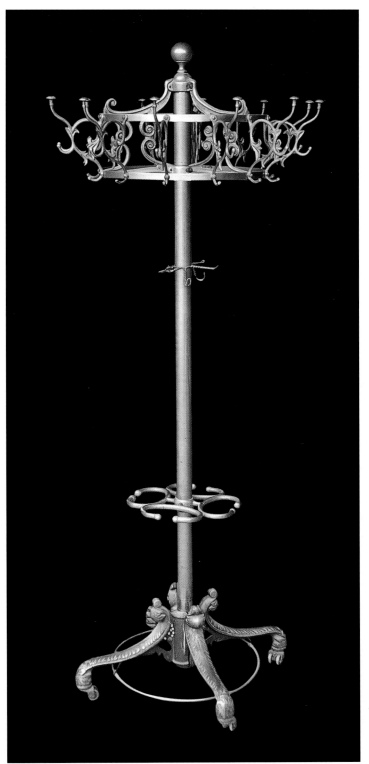

An incredible ornate metal coat and umbrella rack. 75" high. $600-800

A handy and attractive string holder. Given to stores by the companies, they proved to be inexpensive advertising lures for customers. $1000-1200

Two level display stand. Wood and wire. 37" high. $100-125

Two examples of common, everyday string holders. Each $75 -100

A most useful tool of the trade. Footstool for shoe salesman, "Beacon Shoes." Wood and metal. 15" high. $100-150

Cheese cover. Edward R. Smith, Oshkosh, Wisconsin. Wood base, glass cover, sheet metal and cast iron stand. Overall height: 40.5". Glass cover: 7" h x 15" diameter. $75-100

Display rack for Bissell carpet sweepers. Wood. 68" x 18". $200-300

Carpet Sweeper, roller bearing. Bissell's Hall. 47" x 25.5". $100-200

58

Display of a more common sweeper, the ordinary broom. The actual display rack is worth more to a collector than the broom, but as a grouping it really stands out.

Another display of brooms with a true country look to the handles.

Display of wisk brooms and fly swatters.

The storekeeper's broom. An authentic touch to the Bob Lyons country store.

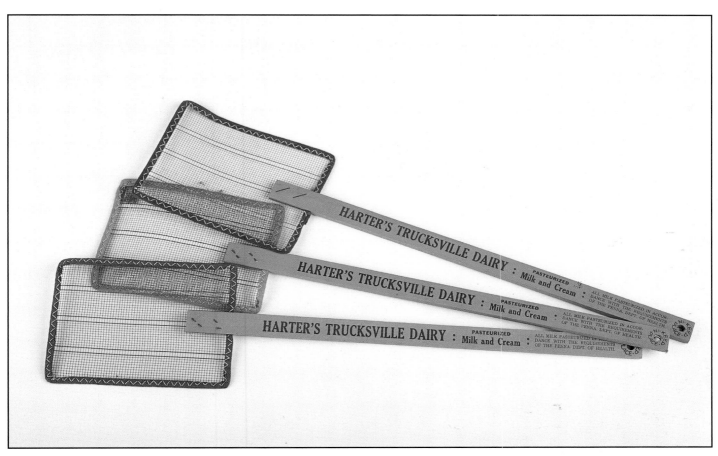

These fly swatters were probably ad giveaways from a distributor and very useful to the storekeeper. $10-20 each, more if advertising is unique or bold.

A great patriotic display for holiday barbeques or a returning soldier's welcome home party. This stand measures 28" Complete with flags $150-200

Another flag display with ornate cast iron base. These have been seen with heavily embossed advertising which could add a few hundred to the price. $75-125.

Selecting a post card was easy, mailing it might have taken considerably longer from rural America. Wooden postcard display rack. 42" high. $200-300

Metal cauldron, 23 gallon capacity, with painted cattle heads. Kenwood, The Wehrle Company, Makers, Newark, Ohio. 31" high" x 28" dia. A great country store example, $4000-4500

A smaller sort of cauldron, made for the handy man of course. Eagle Patching Plaster, 11" x 7". Prices for unique items like this are not consistent, but they are growing in popularity as a whole new "country trades" field is growing.

The common spittoon in some uncommon shapes. Many contained advertising embossed on the sides and are very collectible. These are priced from $75-200

Hanging kerosene lamps. A familiar item sold before the days of the all electric household. $200-300

Tiered kerosene chandelier found in a more affluent home . Metal and glass. Approximately 45" diameter. $1500-2500

A most needed item for any household using kerosene lamps as a light source. Instantaneous Fire Extinguisher, "Bull Dog Brand." The Co-operative Manufacturing Co., Omaha, Nebraska. 22" high. $75-150

Today's home improvement stores still use a form of this display. Graduated screw dispenser. H. Westphal, Pat. Aug 18, 1874, Joliet, Ill. Cast iron. 30" h. Unique item

Assortment of household hardware, including drawer pulls, hinges, and hooks.

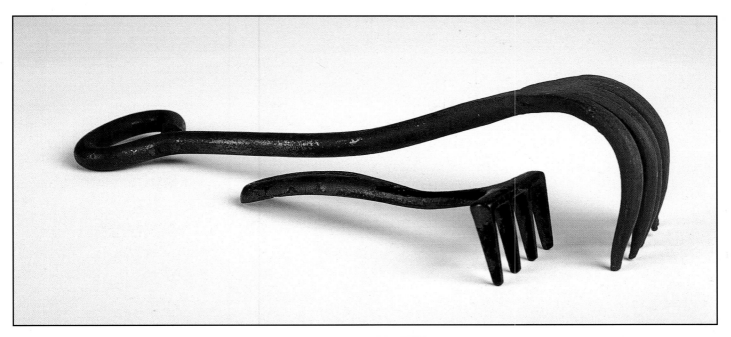

Forged steel rakes for scraping or prying. $35-50

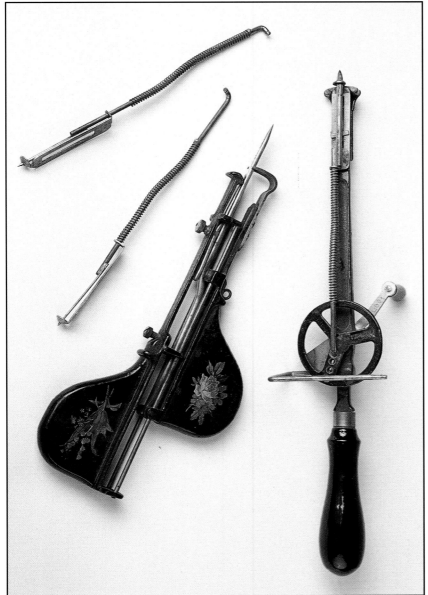

These were probably used in kitchen peeling duties. They are quite ornate and well decorated overall. Collectors today showcase complete collections of these implements on walls lining kitchens and dining rooms. Prices vary according to condition and detail to decals or paint. $25+

Brass spigots and nozzles. People who outfit their homes with authentic appliances make short supply of these old fashioned hardware items. Have seen these sell for $10 to $40+ when the customer really needed to have it.

Remember the kerosene lamps? What better way to avoid spills when filling them constantly! $50+

Assorted pans for the modern kitchen. Molded cake pans bring considerably more than sifters or common pans. Recent sale had plenty of groupings selling from $25 and up.

Candle molds, approximately $10.

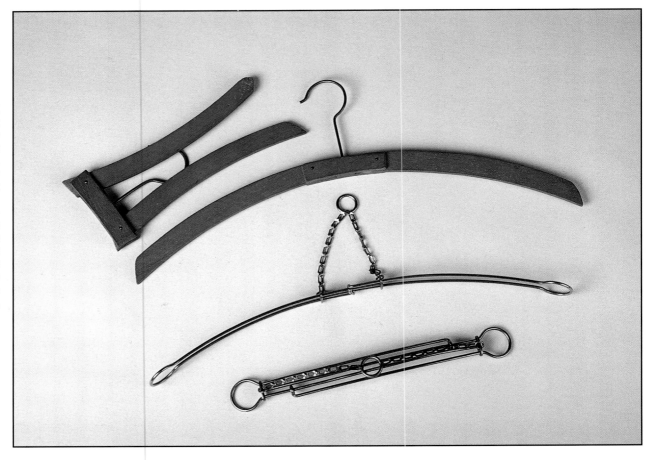

The well-stocked store made it possible to buy every convenience for the home, regardless of how inconsequential it may have seemed. Coat hangers, $5 - 15. Have seen some very early examples sell in the hundreds of dollars, and they make a truly interesting collection.

Salesman's sample for cast iron stove, marked "Phillips & Buttorff Mf'g Co., Nashville, Tenn. 35" x 22.5" x 12". Placing your order for the true scale model made easy for the shopkeeper to save space, and saved him money on expensive inventory. These are highly collectible, recent auction prices $500+. A record price for a sample was set at (Bertoia Auctions) over $20,000.

Salesman's sample for cast iron stove,
marked "Buck's Stoves & Ranges."
13.5" x 14.5" x 8".

True scale cast iron pot belly stoves. Forest City Oak, "13." 40" to 70" high. Many of these are best
restored and renickeled for displaying. These are in great shape for their age, and very ornate. $1000+

Undecided whether to invest in a new range for the Mrs. ? Call a friend with the new public phone telephone. Williams, Electric Co., Cleveland, Ohio. Mahogany. 31" x 16" x 8". $200+

A store with a piano - now that's class! Note the bright tobacco advertising sign in plain sight of the customer. A subliminal suggestion, and probably very effective in its day.

A game of chess always relaxes the customers. At the country store you can play on the house board…or buy one for your home. Family boards, cardboard, depending on advertising $45-75

This carved wooden Indian woman would have looked great on the piano or any counter top. 38" high. $4500-5000

Time to wrap up the goodies in this chapter, and here is the perfect string holder to do the job. Round cast iron string holder with embossed face on top. Cast iron. 7. 5" h., 6" diameter. $500+

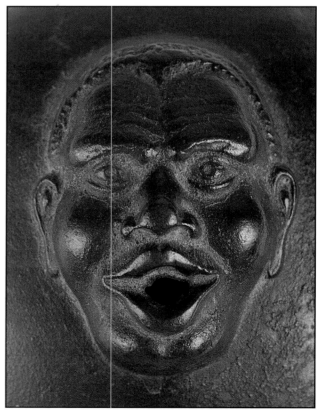

Chapter Three

Clothing for All Occasions

Styles may change over the years, but human nature hasn't changed that much. Everybody still wants to look his or her best, and keep up with the latest in clothing fashion. It may be a little more relaxed today, but people, to a degree, generally still judge people by the clothes they wear, and the way they keep them looking fresh. The country store became a place where the latest in fashion, both from America, and Europe, made many an eye widen with that "have to have it" look. Many of the small town folk had to do business from time to time in the cities, and the country store was just the place to help them dress for success. Whether it was the yearly fair, town dance, a sporting event, or a short business jaunt, the storekeeper was the person to see for all the clothing needs.

The Bob Lyons store has preserved many of those, almost laughable, styles for us today, and this is one of the most interesting of collectibles today. From "head to toe," might have been a great subtitle, as you will soon see, for this curious chapter.

The well dressed country man. Quite a model to emulate, and a full 66" high. $3000+

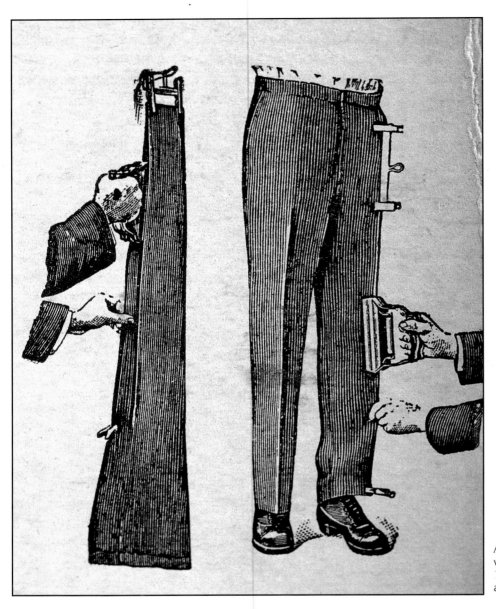

A couple of advertising signs to make the want-to-be-well-dressed man decide. Sign, 17" x 8.5", paper. Knox the Hatter, spring and summer hat catalog, 1888. $200-300

Reverse glass signs gave an air of importance to the haberdashery department. This pair, framed and gilded in gold, sell for approximately $300 each

Spittoon or trade stimulator, it was the keeper's call. This one was in the shape of a top hat. Ceramic, 7", unique

A great snapshot of the incredible clothing department. It looks inviting and arranged as if untouched for many years.

An assortment of hats for any occasion, complete with the original hat stand.

These Panama, or city hats, were quite popular in their day. In fact, they are still worn today, demonstrating that good style never goes out of fashion. $50-75 each

Bowler hats and formal top hats. Many of these were advertised as beaver fur, and command upwards of $75.

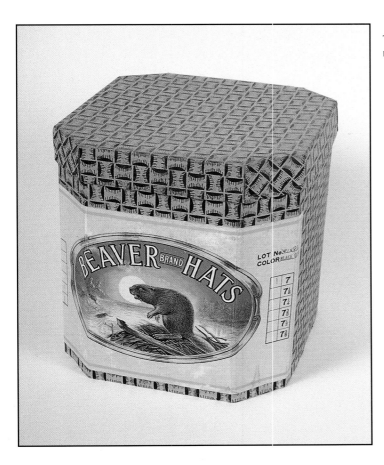

The boxes were colorful and announced the hats with importance.

This advertising mirror, "Gets-It," was a necessity in the shop. 10. 75 h. $100-125

For the kids – a hat that carries the ad when worn. $25

Assortment of straw visor caps, one marked U. S. Customs Inspector, one marked U. S. Post Office Letter Carrier, the third unmarked. A hat for every important town job. $100 -150

A unique and complete display of bow ties. $100.

GENUINE LEATHER

UNIFORM BOW TIE

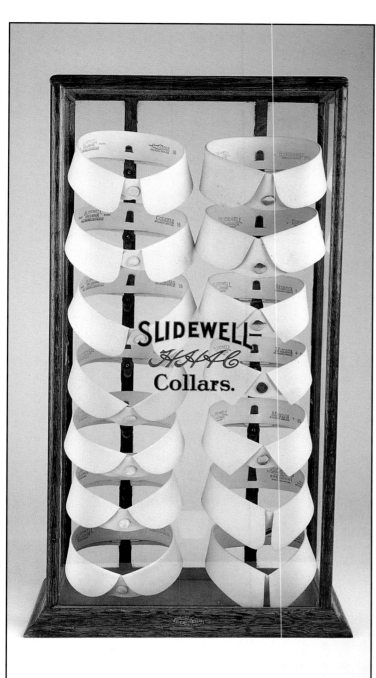

Collar display case. These were very popular and are often found in single, double, or triple rows. $600-750

More formal wear for the man about town. Tuxedo shirt, bow tie, and cuff set. $35-50

Assortment of men's accessories, including gold plated studs, "Itsoezie" Combination Button Cuff Holder, and Glattolin, a product to prevent collars from chafing the neck. $30-50 each

Clothing accessories. Buster Brown's Stockings, Collis' Famous Combination Ankle Supporter for men, Dr. Hawkins Substitute for Suspenders and Belts, Elasticity Waist and Hose Supporters, Arrow Soft Collars, and package of multi-color arm bands. $30-50; depending on box graphics, prices increase.

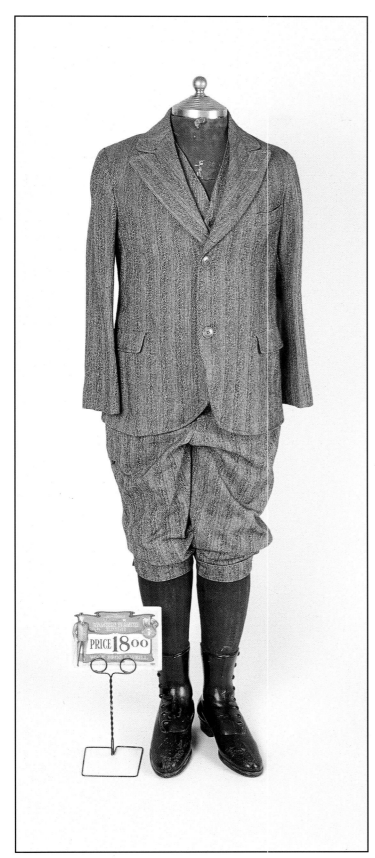

The entire family could walk out of the store dressed to impress even the most important members of the community. I have seen entire suits sell recently for $100-150

One of my favorite ad cases, a real classic. Wooden display cabinet with glass front for "The Sun" Garter. 11" high. $200-300

Straight from the country store shelves. Who said Nehru shirts went out of style. $20-25.

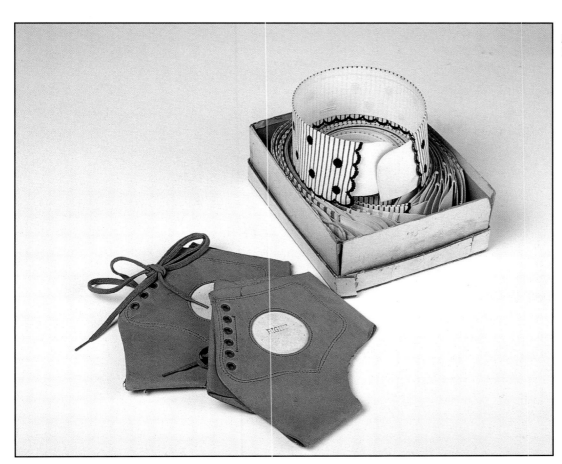

Men's assorted collars; pair of leather spats. $20+

Two pair of men's knickers; two pair of infant pants, including "His First Pair of Pants" from Ritter & Meyer. $25.

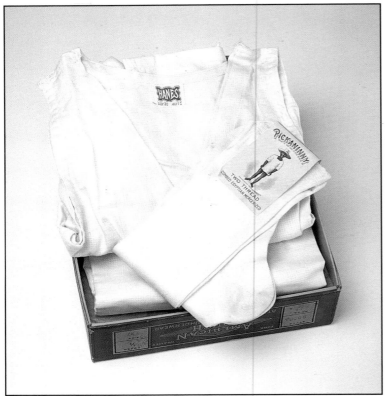

Assorted men's underwear and socks. Value depends upon the beauty of the box more then the original articles of underwear.

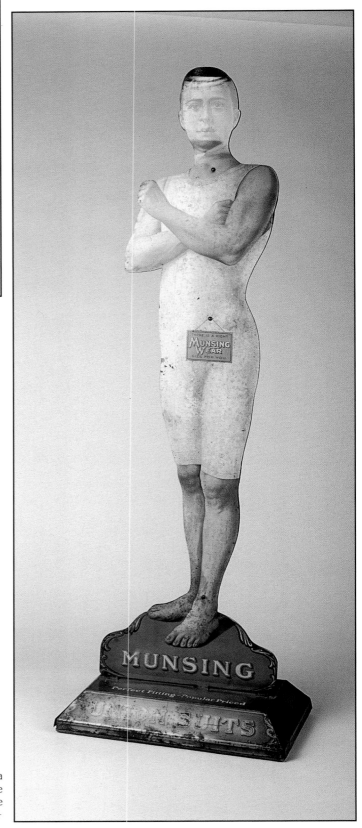

Munsing mannequin advertising Munsing Union Suits, "There is a Right Munsing Wear Size For You." Long union suit shown on one side, short on the other. Lithographed tin. 43" high. Great scale and very desirable tin lithographed die-cut display $2000+

Corsets on display. Fancy laced by skilled hand-workmanship. $35+

91

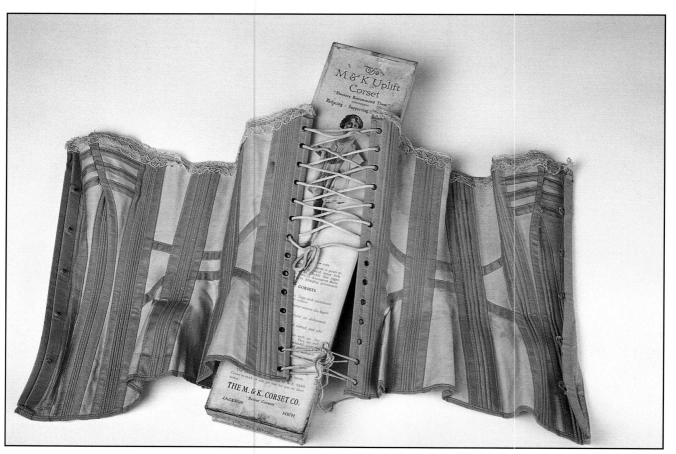

The M & K Uplift Corset, "Doctor's Recommend Them."
The M & K Corset Co., Jackson, Michigan, together with
a typical ad from the 1900's, $30-40 each

Package and three pair of Weldrest Family Tailored Hosiery, Allen Hosiery Company, Philadelphia; package of Sexton Boys' and Girls' Athletic Union Suits; two pairs of Carnation Hosiery "For Men, Women, and Children." $25-55 each

Clockwise from top left: boxes for spats; Oneita Knitted Underwear; Eagle Hard Rubber Combs, and Little Sammie Underwear for Young Americans.

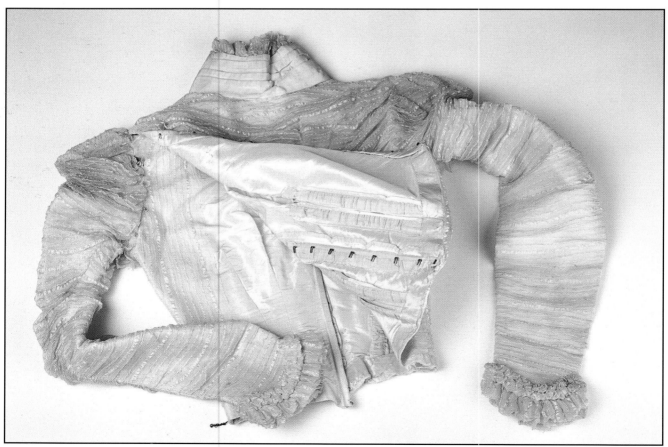

Lace garments for a fancy town dance. $50-75

Dentellières flamandes.

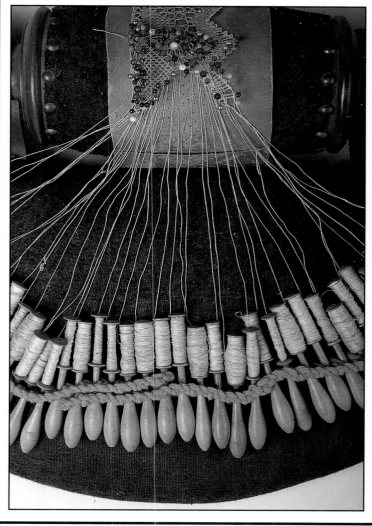

Woman depicted making lace garments, and the equipment needed to create those intricate patterns. This would be a true museum article, quite unique.

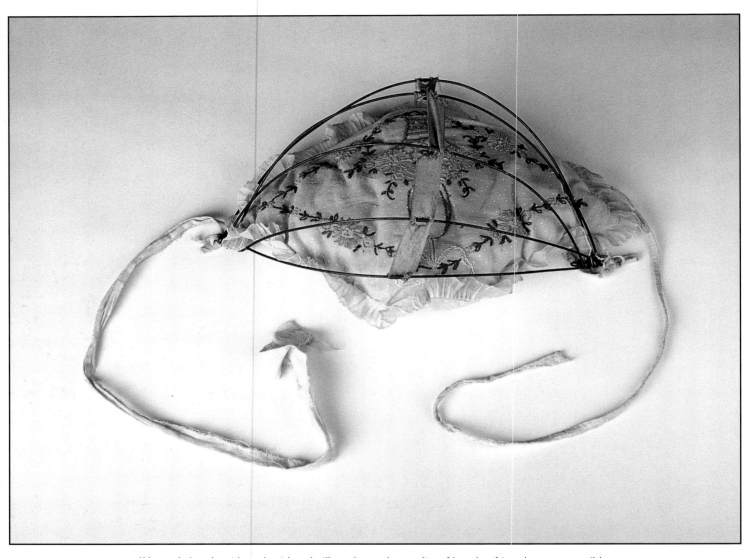

Woman's bustle with embroidered pillow shows the quality of handcrafting that was possible.

Clothing for the casual life of the rich and famous. While prices for these garments can reach the hundreds, knowing that they were once worn by a famous sport star puts them in a different league altogether.

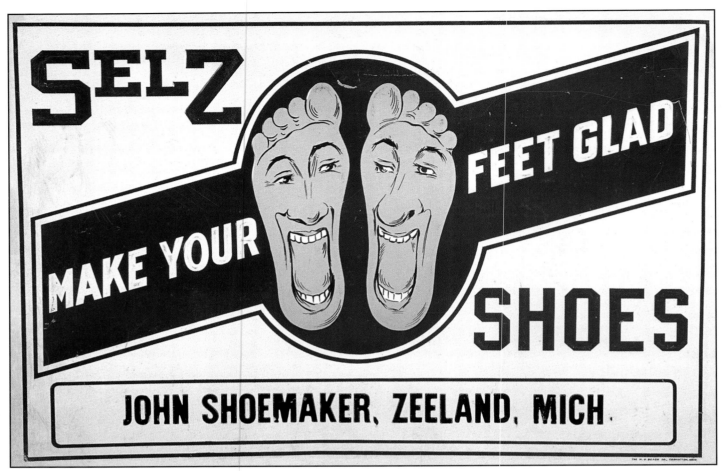

Two signs introducing the footwear
section of the store. $150-200 each

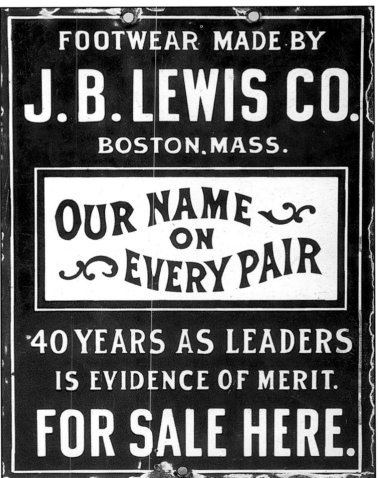

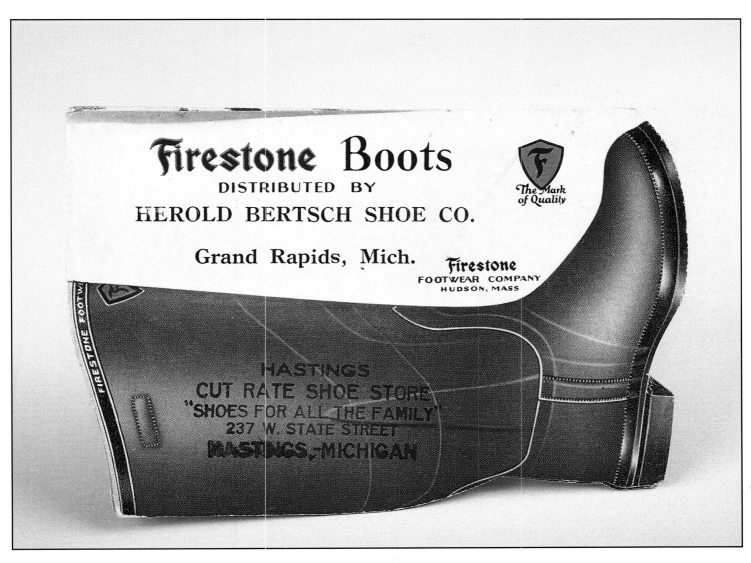

Very visual cardboard boot ad. $300+

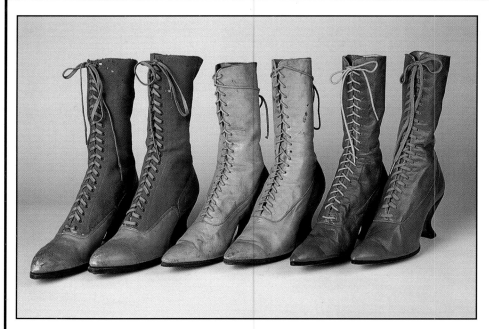

The following entries feature the multi styles of shoes available at a typical store. The selections have always been difficult for women; some things never change. Prices can range from $30 for simple examples to over $100 for full leather lace-up style. Because leather has the tendency to deteriorate over the years, condition and preservation affect pricing considerably for these articles.

Fitting someone with a handicap was no problem. The store could be relied upon for every need. Unique items.

Assorted rubber shoes, including "Ball-Band" Rubber Shoes made by Mishawaka Woolen Mfg. Co., Mishawaka, Indiana, children's hip boots, and men's rubbers. These are more of a museum curiosity than price would dictate.

Men's work boots, or the local firemen's favorite footwear. As a fire collectible they are worth much more. Depending on vintage $100+

"SNAG-PROOF"
TRADE MARK
LAMBERTVILLE RUBBER CO.
TRADE MARK REGISTERED.
LAMBERTVILLE, N.J.
FRANK R. SMITH,
SOMERSET, MICH.,
SOLE AGENT.

A popular and more attractive rubber boot ad sign done in colorful paper lithography. $1500+

RUBBER FOOT WEAR

Advertising that could hang on the ceiling for easy view and optimum store space, shown with actual rubber boot. 33" high. $250-350

Buster Brown
tin litho sign.
Very appealing
and desirable
32.5" high
$5000+

The final touches to the new wardrobe. Gloves, new shoe laces, some fancy cosmetic jewelry, and yes, a touch of rouge from the important looking selection.

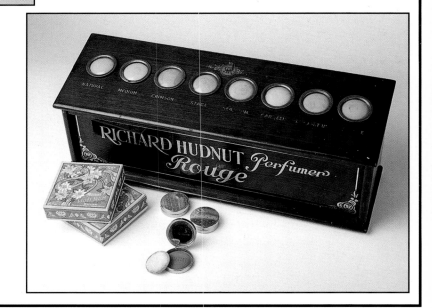

Chapter Four

Stocking the Shelves

Keeping customers happy meant keeping the store chock full of goods. It was literally a one-stop shop, and it must have kept many a storekeeper and his family busy around the clock. Shelves had to remain packed with the latest in medicine, clothing, candy, toys, and, of course, food. Merchandising was a twenty-four hour a day job, but it kept the locals local, and not flocking to the nearest city store. I will highlight but a portion of the enormous variety of store stock Mr. Lyons has amassed over the years, and it might help us realize the true importance of having such a well-stocked store just a short wagon ride from the home.

A period picture of a well stocked country store. Black and white $75-100

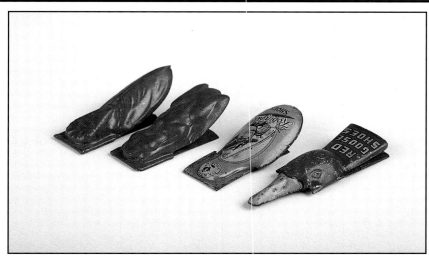

Let's not forget the children. Store shelves usually had their share of amusements for the child in all of us. Toy clickers and horns, and whistle groupings. Many of these were actually given away by shoe, candy, or clothing vendors. $25-75 each

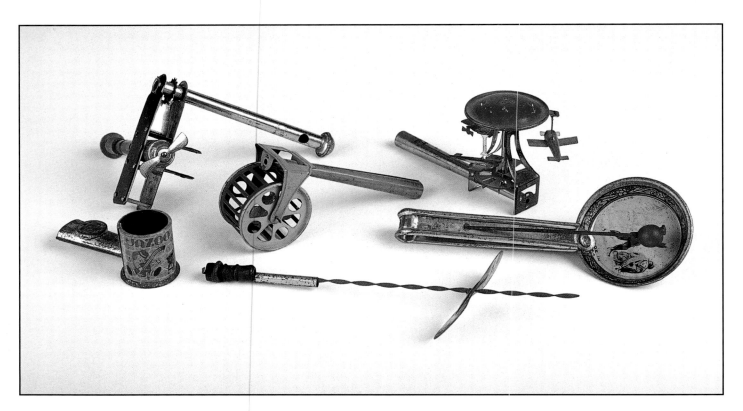

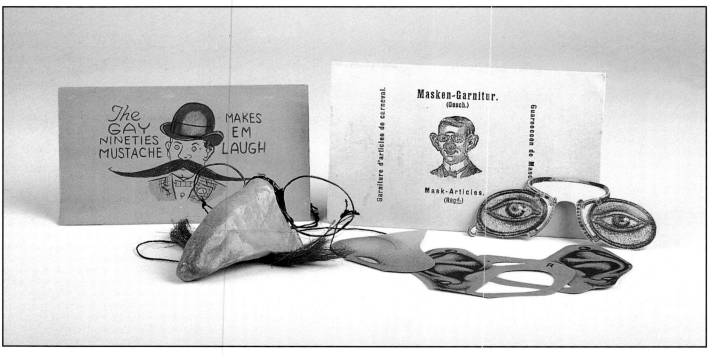

More novelty toys for boys and girls. Whistles, hand held
toys, and disguises. A far cry from today's techno kids.
These toys can range from $100-400

Diminutive delights from American cast iron tools, to the latest in European penny toys. These toys were literally sold for pennies, thus creating the generic badge of honor. Cast iron tools $15 each; penny toys $200-500

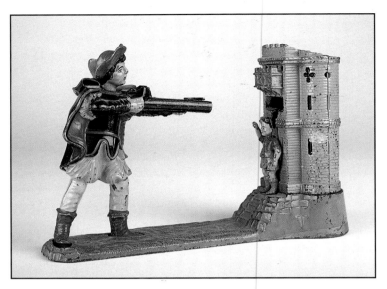

For the really good child, mom or dad may have brought home a wonderful mechanical bank like this William Tell version. $1000-1400, or a tin litho candy vendor still bank, $400-800

And now a look at some really crammed shelves, just waiting to entice faithful customers. Great paper litho boxes with beautiful imagery of women, enough temptation to make anyone want to buy this chewing gum. These gum boxes are in high demand $300+

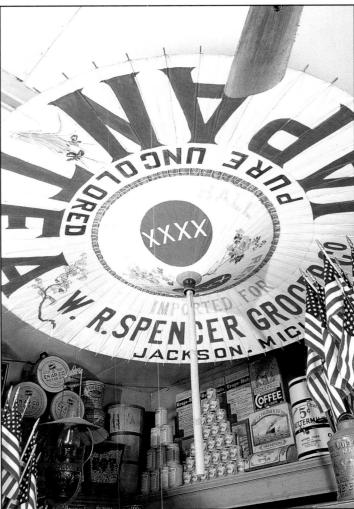

This is a signature shot of Bob's country store. The colorful advertising umbrella hangs high above the remarkably stocked shelves.

Toy Jacks may have been found next to this
large Rye Wafer advertising display box.
Anything to get attention, and it usually worked.
Toys-150; box $300-400

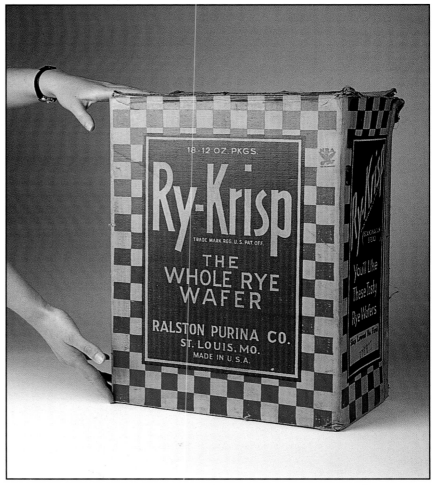

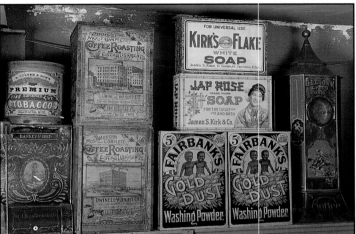

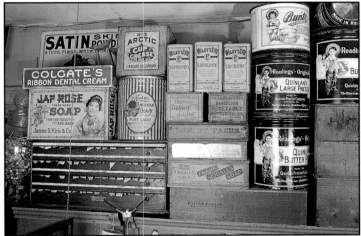

Not an inch of shelf space was wasted in the store that promised to have everything.

An assortment of canned good items. Vegetable cans may be found for $20 and up, while the same holds true for most of the ordinary food items, or cleanser cans. Certain fish products, such as oyster cans, fetch hundreds of dollars, especially the early bail handled variety. Be careful…many of the reproduction paper labels are placed on old stock cans.

For a sweet with therapeutic quality, an assortment of 5 lb. Licorice Lozenge tins. Mellor & Rittenhouse, Philadelphia. Lithographed tin. With glass fronts complete $100-200

For a different sort of acquired sweetness, a display of sweet snuff. $100-150

Tin snuff dispenser. Lithographed tin.
14. 5 h $75-125

And now the real sweet stuff. Honey cans
have become very popular collectibles,
and this includes the really neat ones that
hail from Canada. $75-100

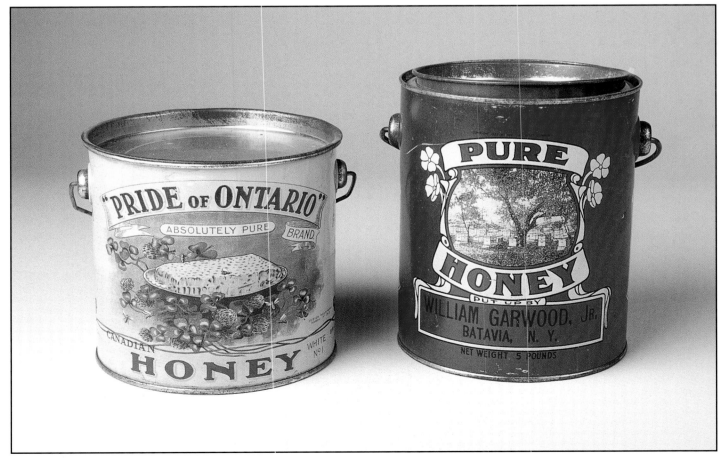

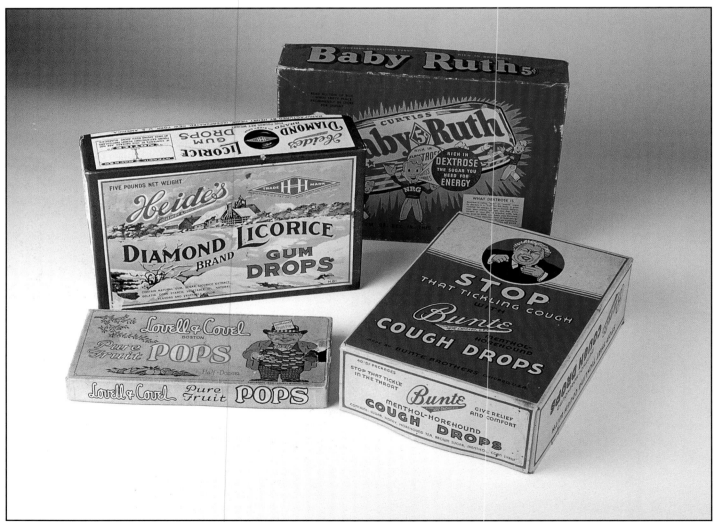

The store contained containers of all sorts, including tin, glass, wood, cardboard and stoneware. Today's markets are still lined with tin cans, but the soldering is not made of lead. While wood and many bottles have been replaced by plastic containers, nothing can replace the colorful, and inexpensive cardboard box. Stoneware jars $300-400; glass jars with candy labels $100-150; and cardboard gum boxes $100-150

118

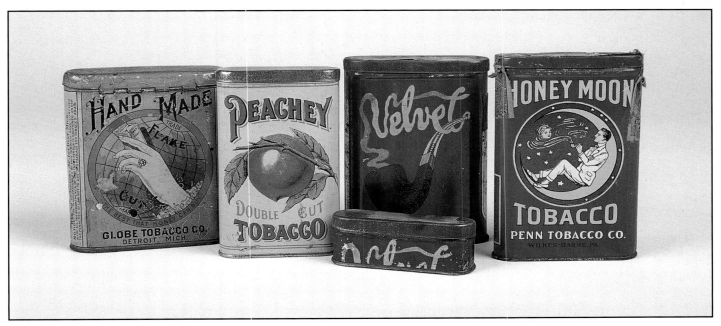

Tobacco products probably made the store more profit than half the other products combined. Hard working men found simple relief in a simple smoke and tobacco companies positioned themselves very hard for a market share. Pictured are four assorted pocket tins, once carried around in a back pocket for a quick fix. $35-300

These handy tobacco packs were cheap and practical on the job. With display $200-300

And a good cup of coffee with that smoke. These milk can style containers are very desirable. $ 300-600

Teas for the ladies. The well stocked shelves carried an inviting selection, all in colorful containers. $25-100

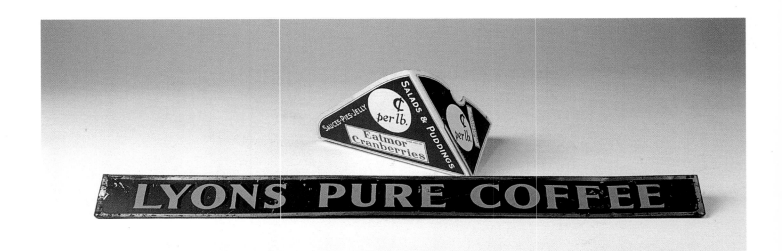

Shelf mountable advertising.
These are priceless to Mr. Lyons

A little spice for the teas . Cylindrical
spice cabinet. 40" high. $400+, this is
rather unique.

121

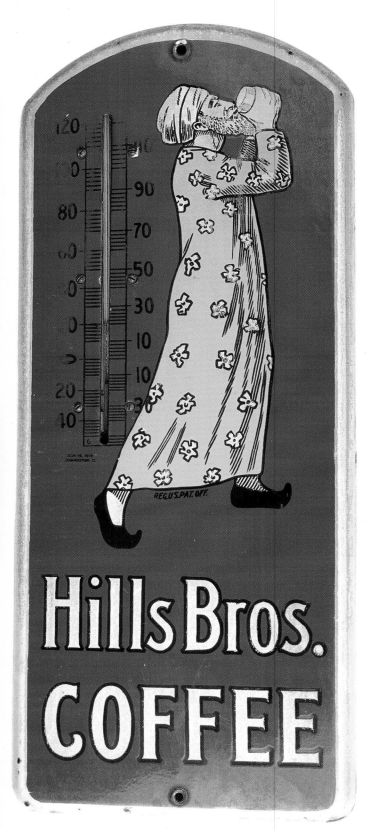

Two great advertising signs for tea and coffee. Porcelain enamel and tin litho images. $500-1500

122

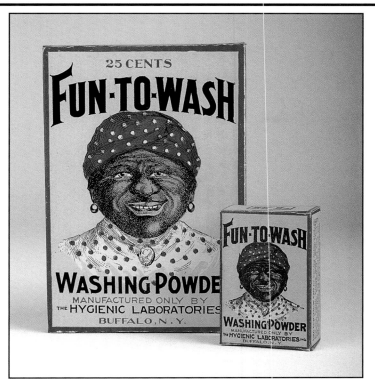

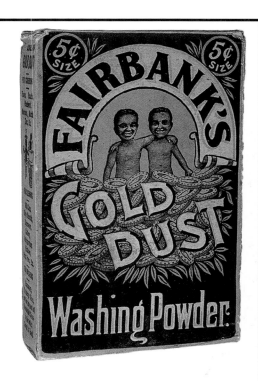

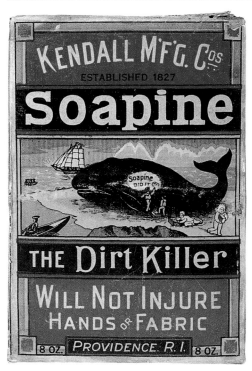

Cleaning products were just as attractively packaged as any other item. Again, the power of paper lithographed imagery and great graphics had buying magnetism. These larger sizes are sometimes incorrectly termed display boxes, but remember, shopping in those days was probably a once a month chore, and larger sizes made it convenient to "bulk" purchase. Color and the graphics share in establishing the price level. $150+ for larger sizes, $50+ for the smaller versions. Starch boxes are not quite as popular yet as soap products. $35-50

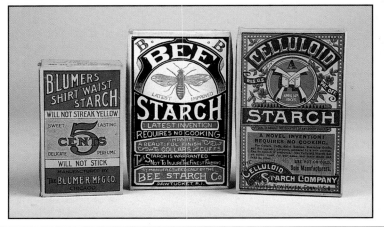

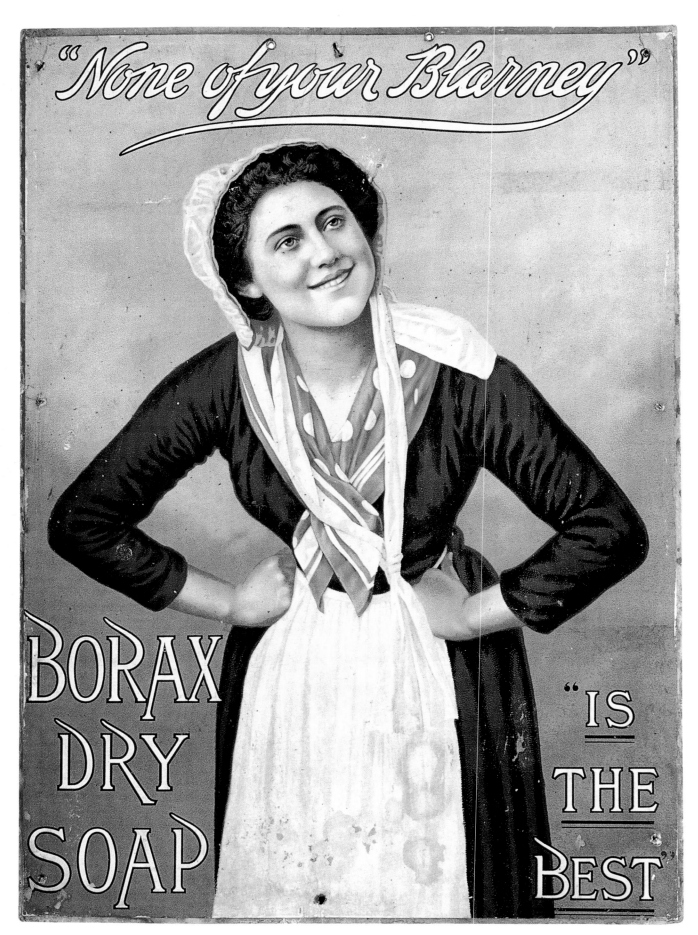

Sign, 17" x 23", cardboard, two-sided Borax Soap. $500-750

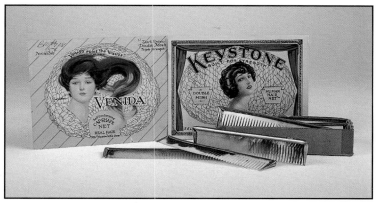

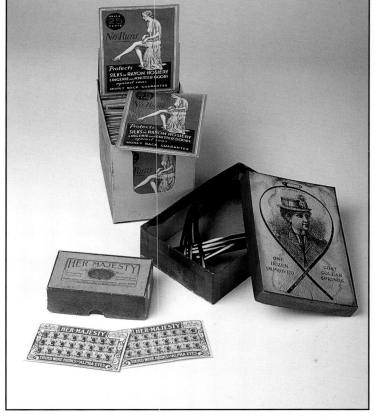

While the men chose their favorite smoke, women fancied their imagination with the latest in look-good products and cosmetics. Talc tins, milk glass lotion jars, and assorted hair products all made a fancy display shelf. These are plentiful in today's market, but still bring $25 and higher for individual items.

A final selection of common country store items that were once on the wish list of every American shopper. Thermos bottles for the working man, large wooden tubs to last for weeks, and assorted household products.

Chapter Five:

Merchandise for the Outdoors

The need to buy food and simple luxuries, such as tobacco and cosmetics, was not the only reason to visit the local country store. People had to make a living and that usually meant feeding the livestock, medicines for the farm animals, mending fences, painting the mayor's home, or anything that could make-up a decent week's wage. Stores sold it all, even if you needed a new farm plow, they could order one for you, and once in a while, people had enough money left over to buy a beautiful wagon for their child or a shiny new harness to show off their horse. The country store was complete with the many products I have termed, " merchandise for the outdoors." These are truly Americana at its best.

Breaking Land in Western Canada at the rate of thirty acres per day.

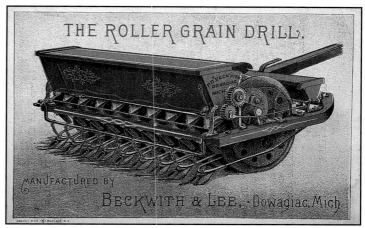

The country store showroom. They could order any one of these farming-made-easier implements for customers. It certainly kept inventory cost down, not to mention the space needed to display them properly. Full color litho images $15-35

A stroll on a sharp looking bike. $1000+

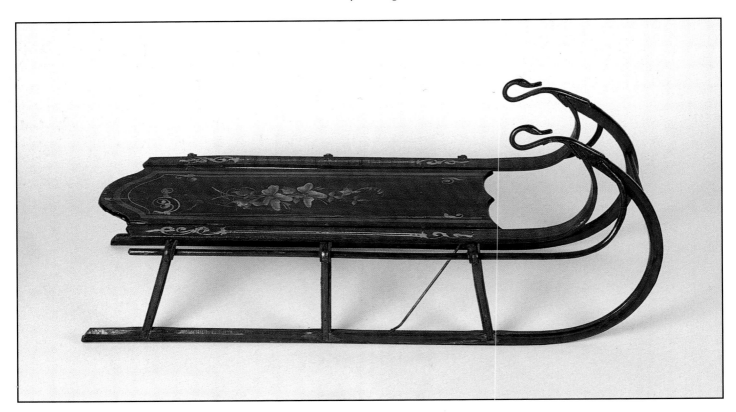

A sled ride in the winter. $500+ depending on scenery painted on the hood.

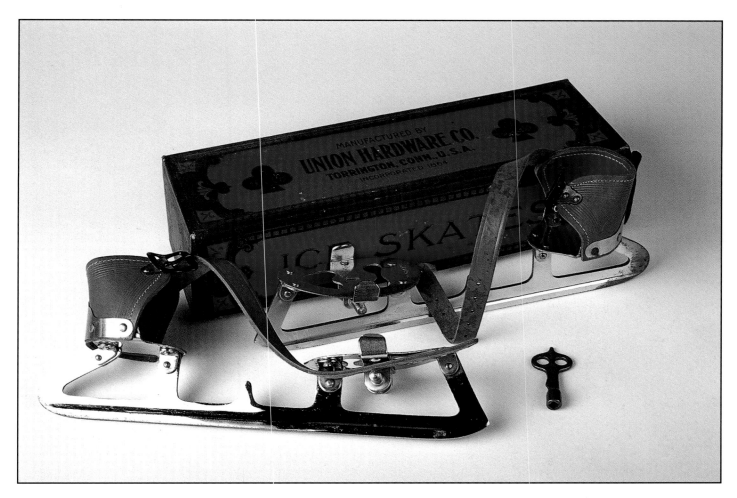

A little skating on the local pond. $50-150

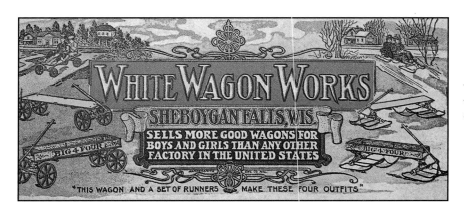

The popularity of the simple wooden wagon is demonstrated by this advertising card. $35

Or a ride on this wagon trail. $250-750

The working men of the community had little time for fun, so it was tools of the trade that caught their attention. These are planters and gardening implements. $150 and up

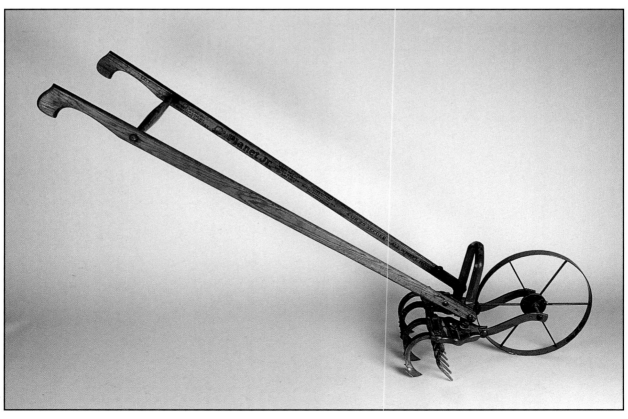

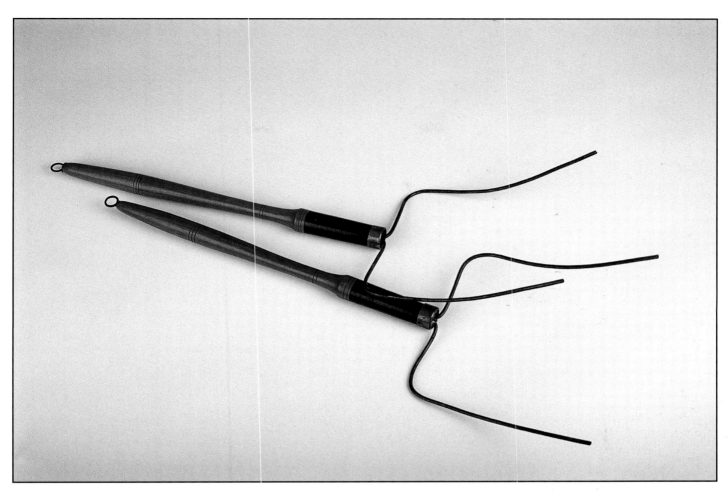

The latest in hay forks might have caused a conversation or two. $25-50

Painting the house or fence in the days before maintenance free siding. $25-50

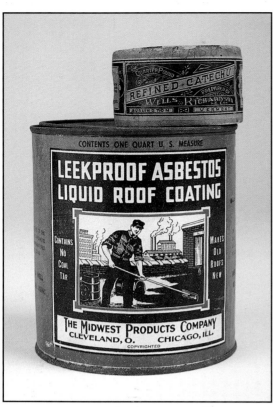

Liquid roof coating, a constant chore for rusty tin roofs. $20-50

Salesman sample stanions for cattle, $800-1200

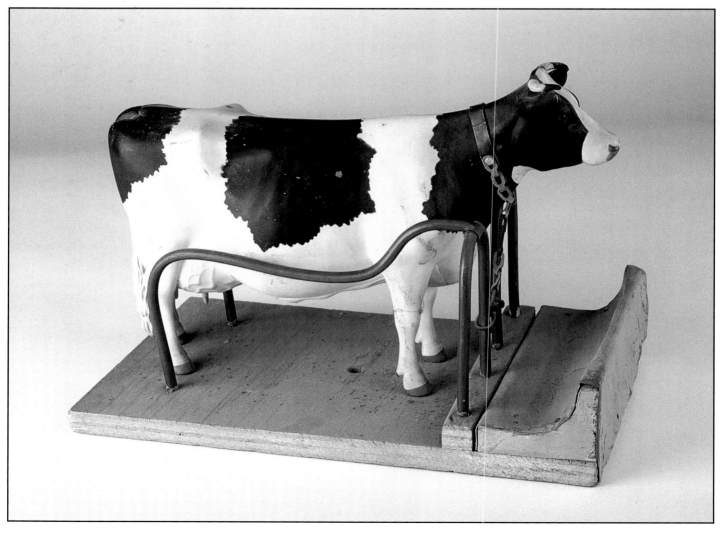

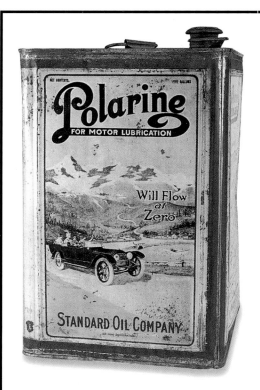

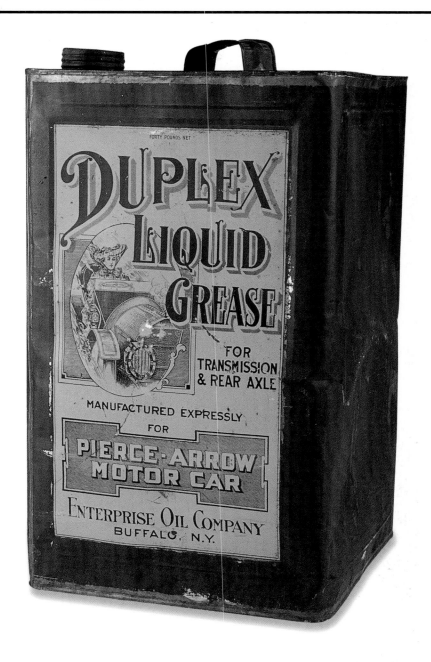

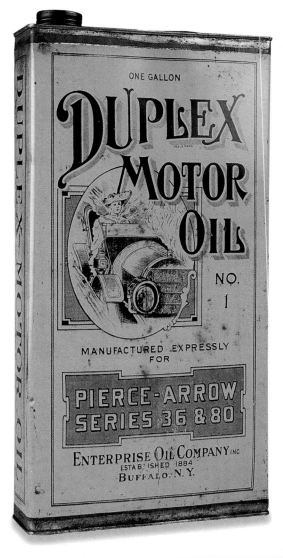

For oil or grease jobs, the store also carried major brands in convenient large tins. These examples are very early and desirable. $300 range

Much earlier versions of oil cans, but
not as graphically appealing. $75-150

Frank Miller's Spring Lubricant and Nut
Loosener, both 16 ozs. The Frank Miller Co.,
New York. Metal. 4.25" h. $35-50

Two examples of shop cans. $100-150

In the country, hunting and fishing was both relaxing and a way to feed a large family. Shell boxes $50-350; tackle sign, $125-250

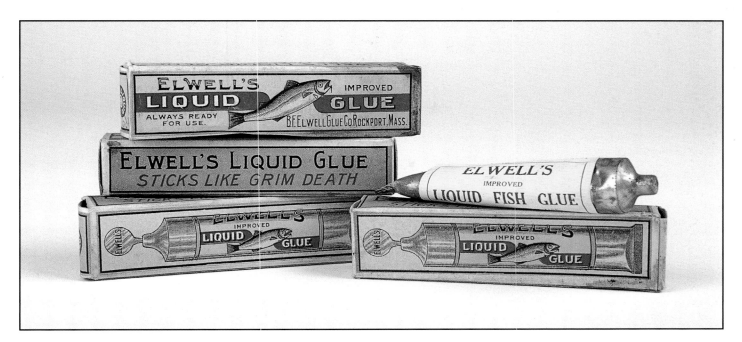

Some glue tubes for every job. $20-40

Batteries for late night hours in a large size reminder display. $250-350

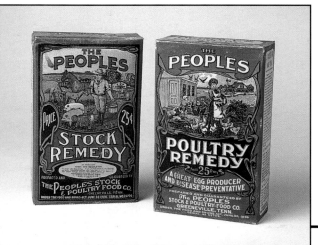

These stock items capture the time capsule of the store preserved for us by Bob Lyons. They include many of the animal cures commonly found in rural areas of the country. Prices range from $35-150, depending on size and cleverness of advertisement.

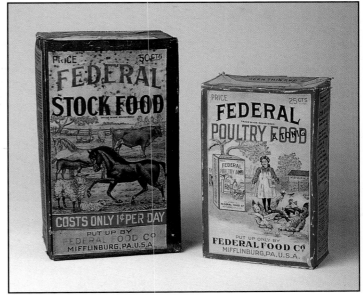

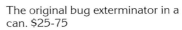
The original bug exterminator in a can. $25-75

Don't ever forget the bait bucket. Great depiction of floating ship, $200-300

Trap of a different sort. Mesh fishing net. $45-75

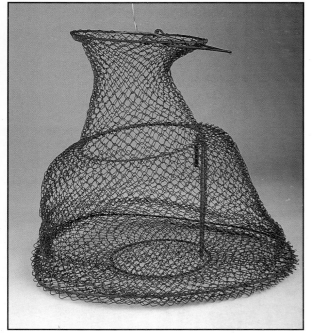

Life is a picnic. Store give-away to a good or lucky client. $75-100

144